The Sea Close By

Albert Camus was born in Algeria in 1913. He studied philosophy at the University of Algiers, then became a journalist, as well as organizing the *Theatre de l'équipe*, a young avant-garde dramatic group. His early essays were collected in *L'Envers et l'endroit* (*The Wrong Side and the Right Side*) and *Noces* (*Nuptials*). As a young man, he went to Paris, where he worked on the newspaper *Paris Soir* before returning to Algiers. His play, *Caligula*, appeared in 1939, while his first two important books, *L'Etranger* (*The Outsider*) and the philosophical essays collected in *Le Mythe de Sisyphe* (*The Myth of Sisyphus*), were published when he returned to Paris. After the occupation of France by the Germans in 1940, Camus became one of the intellectual leaders of the Resistance movement. He edited and contributed to the underground newspaper *Combat*, which he had helped to found. After the war, he devoted himself to writing and established an international reputation with such books as *La Peste* (*The Plague*) (1947), *Les Justes* (*The Just*) (1949) and *La Chute* (*The Fall*) (1956). During the late 1950s, Camus renewed his active interest in the theatre, writing and directing stage adaptations of William Faulkner's *Requiem for a Nun* and Dostoyevsky's *The Possessed*. He was awarded the Nobel Prize for Literature in 1957. Camus was killed in a road accident in 1960. His last novel, *Le Premier Homme* (*The First Man*), unfinished at the time of his death, appeared for the first time in 1994. An instant bestseller, the book received widespread critical acclaim, and has been translated and published in over thirty countries. Much of Camus' work is available in Penguin.

ALBERT CAMUS

The Sea Close By

PENGUIN BOOKS

PENGUIN CLASSICS

Published by the Penguin Group
Penguin Books Ltd, 80 Strand, London WC2R ORL, England
Penguin Group (USA) Inc., 375 Hudson Street, New York, New York 10014, USA
Penguin Group (Canada), 90 Eglinton Avenue East, Suite 700, Toronto, Ontario,
Canada M4P 2Y3 (a division of Pearson Penguin Canada Inc.)
Penguin Ireland, 25 St Stephen's Green, Dublin 2, Ireland
(a division of Penguin Books Ltd)
Penguin Group (Australia), 707 Collins Street, Melbourne, Victoria 3008, Australia
(a division of Pearson Australia Group Pty Ltd)
Penguin Books India Pvt Ltd, 11 Community Centre,
Panchsheel Park, New Delhi – 110 017, India
Penguin Group (NZ), 67 Apollo Drive, Rosedale, Auckland 0632, New Zealand
(a division of Pearson New Zealand Ltd)
Penguin Books (South Africa) (Pty) Ltd, Block D, Rosebank Office Park,
181 Jan Smuts Avenue, Parktown North, Gauteng 2193, South Africa

Penguin Books Ltd, Registered Offices: 80 Strand, London WC2R ORL, England

www.penguin.com

Set in 10.5/13pt Dante MT Std
Typeset by Jouve (UK), Milton Keynes
Printed in Great Britain by Clays Ltd, St Ives plc

ISBN: 978-0-141-39433-6

www.greenpenguin.co.uk

Contents

The Sea Close By

Logbook

I grew up in the sea and poverty was sumptuous, then I lost the sea and found all luxuries grey and poverty unbearable. Since then, I have been waiting. I wait for the homebound ships, the house of the waters, the limpidity of day. I wait patiently, am polite with all my strength. Men see me walk by in fine and learned streets, I admire landscapes, applaud like everyone else, shake hands, but it is not me speaking. Men praise me, I dream a little, they insult me, I scarcely show surprise. Then I forget, and smile at the man who insulted me, or am too courteous in greeting the person I love. What can I do if all I can remember is one image? Finally they call upon me to tell them who I am. 'Nothing yet, nothing yet . . .'

It is at funerals that I excel myself. I do, indeed. I walk slowly through the iron-strewn paths of suburbs, travelling along wide lanes planted with cement trees and leading to holes in the cold earth. There, beneath the scarcely reddening bandage of the sky, I watch bold workmen inter my friends beneath six feet of earth. If I then cast the flower which a clay-covered hand holds out to me, it never misses the grave. My piety is exact, my feelings as they *should be, my head is suitably inclined. I am admired for finding just the right word. But I have no merit in this: I am waiting.*

I have been waiting for a long time. Sometimes, I stumble, I lose my touch, success evades me. What does it matter, for I am then alone. It is thus that I wake up at night, and, still half-asleep, think I hear the sound of waves and the breathing of the waters. Fully awake, I recognize the wind in the trees and the sad murmur of the empty town. I then need all my art to hide my distress or clothe it in the prevailing fashion.

At other times, on the contrary, I am helped. On certain days in New York, lost at the bottom of those wells of stones and steel where wander millions of men, I would run from one to another. without seeing where they ended, exhausted, until I was sustained only by the human mass seeking its way out. But, each time, the distant siren of a tug-boat came to remind me that this town, this empty well, was an island, and at the tip of the Battery the water of my baptism was awaiting me, black and rotting, covered over with hollow corks.

Thus, though I possess nothing, have given away my fortune, camp by the side of all my houses, I can still be blessed with all riches when I choose, set sail at every hour, unknown to despair. There is no country for those who despair, but I know that the sea comes before and after me, and hold my madness ready. Those who love and are separated can live in grief, but this is not despair: they know that love exists. This is why I suffer, dry-eyed, in exile. I am still waiting. A day comes, at last . . .

The bare feet of the sailors beat softly on the deck. It is dawn, and we are setting sail. The moment we leave harbour, a short, gusty wind vigorously brushes the sea which curls backwards in small, foamless waves. A little later the wind freshens and scatters the sea with swiftly vanished camellias. Thus throughout the morning we hear our sails slapping over a cheerful pond. The waters are heavy, scaly, covered with cool foam. From time to time the waves yap against the bow; a bitter, unctuous foam, the God's saliva, flows along the wood and loses itself in the water where it scatters into shapes that die and are reborn, the hide of a white and blue cow, an exhausted beast which drifts a long way behind our wake.

Since our departure the seagulls have been following our ship, apparently without effort, almost without moving their wings. Their fine straight navigation scarcely leans upon the breeze. Suddenly, a loud plop at the level of the kitchens casts a greedy alarm among the birds, throws their fine flight into confusion and sends up a fire of white wings. The seagulls whirl madly in every direction, and then without any loss of speed drop away from the fight one by one and dive down to the sea. A few seconds later they are together again on the water, a quarrelsome farmyard that we leave behind us, nestling in the hollow of the wave, and slowly plucking through the manna of scraps.

At noon, under a deafening sun the sea, exhausted, scarcely finds the strength to rise. When it falls back on itself, it makes the silence whistle. It cooks for an hour and the pale water, a vast white-hot iron sheet sizzles. In a minute it will turn and offer its damp side, now hidden in waves and darkness, to the sun.

We pass by the gates of Hercules, the headland where Antaeus died. Beyond, the Ocean lies everywhere, on one side we pass by the Horn and the Cape of Good Hope, the Meridians wed the Latitudes, the Pacific drinks the Atlantic. Once our course is set for Vancouver, we plunge slowly towards the South Seas. A few cables' lengths away Easter Island, Desolation and the New Hebrides file past us in convoy. Suddenly one morning the seagulls disappear. We are far from any land, and alone, with our sails and our engines.

Alone also with the horizon. The waves come from the invisible East, patiently, one by one; they reach us, and then, patiently, set off again for the unknown West, one by one. A long voyage, with no beginning and no end. . . . Rivers and streams pass by, the sea passes and remains. This is how we must love it, faithful and fleeting. I wed the sea.

The high seas. The sun sinks down, is swallowed by the mists long before it reaches the horizon. For one brief moment, the sea is pink on one side and blue on the other. Then the waters grow darker. The schooner slides, minute, over the surface of a perfect circle of thick, tarnished metal. And at the most peaceful hour, as evening comes, hundreds of porpoises emerge from the water, play around us for a moment, then flee to the horizon where there are no men. They leave behind them the silence and anguish of primitive waters.

A little later still, we meet an iceberg on the Tropic. Doubtless invisible after its long voyage in these warm waters, but still effective: it passes to starboard, where the rigging is briefly covered with a frosty dew, while to port the day dies without moisture.

★

Night does not fall at sea. Rather, from the depths of the waters, which an already submerged sun gradually darkens with its thick ashes, it rises towards the still pale sky. For a brief moment Venus shines alone above the black waves. In the twinkling of an eye, stars swarm in the liquid night.

The moon has risen. First it gently illuminates the surface of the waters, then mounts higher and writes upon the supple water. At last at its zenith it lights up a whole corridor of sea, a rich river of milk which, with the motion of the ship, flows inexhaustibly towards us through the dark ocean. Here is the faithful night, the cool night which I called for amid the noise of lights, drink and the tumult of desire.

We sail across spaces so vast they seem unending. Sun and moon rise and fall in turn, on the same thread of light and night. Days at sea, even and indistinguishable as happiness . . .

This life rebellious to forgetfulness, rebellious to memory, of which Stevenson speaks.

Dawn. We sail perpendicularly across the Tropic of Cancer, the waters groan and are convulsed. Day breaks over a surging sea, full of steel spangles. The sky is white with mist and heat, with a dead but unbearable glare, as if the sun had turned liquid in the thickness of the clouds, over the whole stretch of the celestial vault. A sick sky over a decomposing sea. As the day draws on, the heat grows in the white air. All day long the bow noses out clouds of flying fish, small iron birds, forcing them from their bushes in the waves.

*

In the afternoon we meet a steamer going back towards the towns. Our sirens exchange greetings in three great hoots, like prehistoric animals. Passengers lost at sea are warned that other men are present and exchange greetings with them, the two ships draw slowly farther apart upon the malevolent waters; all this fills the heart with sadness. What man who cherishes the sea and loneliness will ever stop himself from loving these obstinate madmen who, clinging to planks and tossed by the mane of immense oceans, chase after islands long adrift?

In the very midst of the Atlantic we bend beneath savage winds blowing endlessly from pole to pole. Each cry we utter is lost, flies off into limitless space. But this cry, carried day after day on the winds, will finally reach land at one of the flattened ends of the earth and echo timelessly against the frozen walls until a man, lost somewhere in his shell of snow, hears it and consents to smile with happiness.

I was half asleep in the early afternoon sun when a terrible noise awoke me. I saw the sun in the depths of the sea, the waves reigning in the surging heavens. Suddenly the sea was alight, the sun flowed in long icy draughts down my throat. Around me the sailors were laughing and crying. They loved one another, yet with no forgiveness. On that day I recognized the world for what it was, I consented that its good should also do evil and its drawback carry benefits. On that day I realized that there were two truths, of which one must never be told.

★

The curious Austral moon, slightly pared, accompanies us for several nights and then slides rapidly from the sky down to the sea which swallows it. There remains the Southern Cross, the infrequent stars, the porous air. At the same instant, the wind also ceases completely. The sky rolls and pitches above our immobile masts. Engine dead, sails hove to, we whistle in the warm night while the water beats amicably against our sides. No commands, the machines are silent. Why indeed should we carry on and why should we return? Our cup runneth over, and a mute, invincible madness rocks us to sleep. A day comes like this which draws everything to a close; we must then let ourselves sink, like those who swim until exhausted. What do we accomplish? For ever, I have held it secret from myself. O bitter bed, princely couch, the crown lies at the bottom of the seas.

In the morning the lukewarm water foams gently under our propeller. We put on speed. Towards noon, travelling from distant continents, a herd of sea cows cross our path, overtake us and swim rhythmically northwards, followed by multicoloured birds which, from time to time, rest upon their horns. This rustling forest slowly vanishes on the horizon. A little later, the sea is covered over with strange, yellow flowers. Towards evening, for hour after hour, we are preceded by an invisible song. I go to sleep, at home.

All our sails stretched in a keen breeze, we race across a clear and rippling sea. At top speed our helm goes hard to port. And towards nightfall, correcting our course again, listing so far to starboard that our sails skim the water, we sail rapidly along the side of a southern continent which I recognize for having in former days flown blindly across it in the barbarous coffin of an aeroplane. I was an idle king and my chariot dawdled; I waited for the sea but it never came. The monster roared, took off from the guano fields of Peru, hurled itself above the beaches of the Pacific, flew over the fractured white vertebrae of the Andes and then above the herds of flies which cover the immense Argentinian plain, linked with one swoop the milk-flowing Uruguyan meadows to the black rivers of Venezuela, landed, roared again, quivered with greed at the sight of new empty spaces to devour, and yet never ceased failing to move forward or at least did so only with a convulsed, obstinate slowness, a fixed, weary and intoxicated energy. I felt then that I was dying in my metallic cell and dreamed of bloodshed and of orgies. Without space there is neither innocence nor liberty! When a man cannot breathe, prison means death or madness; what can he do there but kill and possess? Today, on the contrary, I have all the air I need, all our sails slap in the blue air, I am going to cry out with speed, we throw our sextants and compasses into the sea.

Under the imperious wind our sails are like iron. The coast drifts at full speed before our eyes, forests of royal coconut trees whose feet are bathed by emerald lagoons, a quiet bay, full of red sails, moonlit beaches. Great buildings loom up, already cracking under the pressure of the virgin forest which begins in the servants' courtyard; here and there a yellow ipeca or a tree with violet branches burst through a window, Rio finally crumbles away behind us and the monkeys of Tijuca will laugh and gibber in the vegetation that has overgrown its new ruins. Still faster, along wide beaches where the waves spread out in sheaves of sand, still faster, where the Uruguyan sheep plunge into the sea and at once turn it yellow. Then on the Argentinian coast great crude piles of faggots, set up at regular intervals, raise slowly grilling halves of oxen to the sky. At night the ice from Tierra del Fuego comes and beats for hours against our hull; the ship barely loses speed and tacks about. In the morning the single wave of the Pacific, whose cold foam boils green and white for thousands of kilometres along the Chilean coast, slowly lifts us up and threatens to wreck us. The helm avoids it, overtakes the Kerguelen Islands. In the sweetish evening the first Malayan ships come out to meet us.

'To sea! To sea!' shouted the magical boys in one of my childhood books. I have forgotten everything of the book except this cry. 'To sea!', and from across the Indian Ocean to the banks of the Red Sea, where in the silent nights you can hear the stones in the desert, scorched in the daytime, cracking one by one, we come back to the antique sea in which all cries are hushed.

Finally one morning we drop anchor in a bay filled with a strange silence, beaconed with fixed sails. All we can see are a few sea birds quarrelling in the sky over scraps of reeds. We swim ashore to an empty beach; we spend all day swimming and drying ourselves in the sand. When evening comes, under a sky that turns green and fades into the distance, the sea, so calm already, becomes still more peaceful. Short waves blow a vaporous foam on to the lukewarm shore. The sea birds have disappeared. All that is left is a space, lying open to a motionless voyage.

The knowledge that certain nights of prolonged gentleness will return to the earth and sea when we have gone can indeed help us in our death. Vast sea, forever virgin and forever ploughed, my religion with the night! It washes and feeds us in its sterile furrows, frees us and holds us upright. Each wave brings its promise, always the same. What does the wave say? If I were to die, in the midst of cold mountains, unknown to the world, cast off by my own people, my strength at last exhausted, the sea would at the final moment flood into my cell, come to raise me above myself and help me die without hatred.

At midnight, alone on the shore. One moment more and then I shall set sail. The sky itself has weighed anchor, with all its stars, like those ships which at this very hour gleam throughout the world with all their lights and illuminate dark harbour waters. Space and silence weigh equally upon the heart. A sudden love, a great work, a decisive act, a thought which transfigures, all these at certain moments bring the same unbearable anxiety, linked with an irresistible charm. Is living like this in the delicious anguish of being, in exquisite proximity to a danger whose name we do not know the same as rushing to our doom? Once again, without respite, let us go.

I have always felt that I was living on the high seas, threatened, at the heart of a royal happiness.

Summer in Algiers

For Jacques Heurgon

The loves we share with a city are often secret loves. Old walled towns like Paris, Prague, and even Florence are closed in on themselves and hence limit the world that belongs to them. But Algiers (together with certain other privileged places such as cities on the sea) opens to the sky like a mouth or a wound. In Algiers one loves the commonplace: the sea at the end of every street, a certain volume of sunlight, the beauty of the race. And, as always, in that unashamed offering there is a secret fragrance. In Paris it is possible to be homesick for space and a beating of wings. Here, at least, man is gratified in every wish and, sure of his desires, can at last measure his possessions.

Probably one has to live in Algiers for some time in order to realize how paralysing an excess of nature's bounty can be. There is nothing here for whoever would learn, educate himself, or better himself. This country has no lessons to teach. It neither promises nor affords glimpses. It is satisfied to give, but in abundance. It is completely accessible to the eyes, and you know it the moment you enjoy it. Its pleasures are without remedy and its joys without hope.

Above all, it requires clairvoyant souls – that is, without solace. It insists upon one's performing an act of lucidity as one performs an act of faith. Strange country that gives the man it nourishes both his splendour and his misery! It is not surprising that the sensual riches granted to a sensitive man of these regions should coincide with the most extreme destitution. No truth fails to carry with it its bitterness. How can one be surprised, then, if I never feel more affection for the face of this country than amidst its poorest men?

During their entire youth men find here a life in proportion to their beauty. Then, later on, the downhill slope and obscurity. They wagered on the flesh, but knowing they were to lose. In Algiers whoever is young and alive finds sanctuary and occasion for triumphs everywhere: in the bay, the sun, the red and white games on the seaward terraces, the flowers and sports stadiums, the cool-legged girls. But for whoever has lost his youth there is nothing to cling to and nowhere where melancholy can escape itself. Elsewhere, Italian terraces, European cloisters, or the profile of the Provençal hills – all places where man can flee his humanity and gently liberate himself from himself. But everything here calls for solitude and the blood of young men. Goethe on his deathbed calls for light and this is a historic remark. At Belcourt and Bab-el-Oued old men seated in the depths of cafés listen to the bragging of young men with plastered hair.

Summer betrays these beginnings and ends to us in Algiers. During those months the city is deserted. But the poor remain and the sky. We join the former as they go down towards the harbour and man's treasures: warmth of the water and the brown bodies of women. In the evening, sated with such wealth, they return to the oilcloth and kerosene-lamp that constitute the whole setting of their life.

In Algiers no one says 'go for a swim' but rather 'indulge in a swim'. The implications are clear. People swim in the harbour and go to rest on the buoys. Anyone who passes near a buoy where a pretty girl is sunning herself shouts to his friends: 'I tell you it's a seagull.' These are healthy amusements. They must obviously constitute the ideal of those youths since most of them continue the same life in the winter, undressing every day at noon for a frugal lunch in the sun. Not that they have read the boring sermons of the nudists, those Protestants of the flesh (there is a theory of the body quite as tiresome as that of the mind). But they are simply 'comfortable in the sunlight'. The importance of this custom for our epoch can never be overestimated. For the first time in two thousand years the body has appeared naked on beaches. For twenty centuries men have striven to give decency to Greek insolence and *naïveté*, to diminish the flesh and complicate dress. Today, despite that history, young men running on Mediterranean beaches repeat the gestures of the athletes of Delos. And living thus among bodies and through one's body one becomes aware that it has its connotations, its life and, to risk nonsense, a psychology of its own.* The body's evolution, like that of the

---

* May I take the ridiculous position of saying that I do not like the way Gide exalts the body? He asks it to restrain its desire to make it keener. Thus he comes dangerously near to those who in brothel-slang are called involved or brainworkers. Christianity also wants to suspend desire. But, more natural, it sees a mortification in this. My friend, Vincent, who is a cooper and junior breast-stroke champion, has an even clearer view. He

mind, has its history, its vicissitudes, its progress and its defi-
ciency. With this distinction, however: colour. When you
frequent the beach in summer you become aware of a sim-
ultaneous progression of all skins from white to golden to
tanned, ending up in a tobacco-colour which marks the
extreme limit of the effort of transformation of which the
body is capable. Above the harbour stands the set of white
cubes of the Kasbah. When you are at water-level, against
the sharp white background of the Arab town the bodies
describe a copper-coloured frieze. And, as the month of
August progresses and the sun grows, the white of the
houses becomes more blinding and skins take on a darker
warmth. How can one fail to participate then in that dia-
logue of stone and flesh in tune with the sun and seasons?
The whole morning has been spent in diving, in bursts of
laughter amid splashing water, in vigorous paddles around
the red and black freighters (those from Norway with all
the scents of wood, those that come from Germany full
of the smell of oil, those that go up and down the coast
and smell of wine and old casks). At the hour when the
sun overflows from every corner of the sky at once, the
orange canoe loaded with brown bodies brings us home in
a mad race. And when, having suddenly interrupted the
cadenced beat of the double paddle's bright-coloured wings,
we glide slowly in the calm water of the inner harbour, how
can I fail to feel that I am piloting through the smooth

---

drinks when he is thirsty, if he desires a woman tries to go to bed with her,
and would marry her if he loved her (this hasn't yet happened). Afterwards he always says: 'I feel better' – and this sums up vigorously any
apology that might be made for satiety.

waters a savage cargo of gods, in whom I recognize my brothers?

But at the other end of the city summer is already offering us by way of contrast its other riches: I mean its silences and its boredom. That silence is not always of the same quality, depending on whether it springs from the shade or the sunlight. There is the silence of noon on the Place du Gouvernement. In the shade of the trees surrounding it Arabs sell for five sous glasses of iced lemonade flavoured with orange-flowers. Their cry 'Cool, cool', can be heard across the empty square. After their cry silence again falls under the burning sun: in the vendor's jug the ice moves and I can hear its tinkle. There is the silence of the siesta. In the streets of the Marine, in front of the dirty barber shops it can be measured in the melodious buzzing of flies behind the hollow reed curtains. Elsewhere, in the Moorish cafés of the Kasbah the body is silent, unable to tear itself away, to leave the glass of tea and rediscover time with the pulsing of its own blood. But, above all, there is the silence of summer evenings.

Those brief moments when day topples into night must be peopled with secret signs and summonses for my Algiers to be so closely linked to them. When I spend some time far from that town, I imagine its twilights as promises of happiness. On the hills above the city there are paths among the mastics and olive-trees. And towards them my heart turns at such moments. I see flights of black birds rise against the green horizon. In the sky suddenly divested of its sun something relaxes. A whole little nation of red clouds stretches out until it is absorbed in the air. Almost immediately afterwards appears the first star that had been seen taking shape and consistency in the depth of the sky. And then suddenly, all consuming, night. What exceptional quality do the fugitive Algerian evenings possess to be able to release so many things in me? I haven't time to tire of that sweetness they leave on my lips before it has disappeared into night. Is this the secret of its persistence? This country's affection is overwhelming and furtive. But during the moment it is present one's heart at least surrenders completely to it. At Padovani Beach the dance hall is open every day. And in that huge rectangular box with its entire side open to the sea, the poor young people of the neighbourhood dance until evening. Often I used to await there a moment of exceptional beauty. During the day the hall is protected by sloping wooden awnings. When the sun goes down they are raised. Then the hall is filled with an odd green light born of the double shell of the sky and the sea. When one is seated far from the windows, one sees only the sky and, silhouetted against it, the faces of the dancers passing in succession. Sometimes a waltz is being played and, against the green background, the black profiles whirl obstinately like those cut-out silhouettes that are attached to a phonograph's turntable. Night comes rapidly after this and with it the lights. But I am unable to relate the thrill and secrecy that subtle instant holds for me. I recall at least a magnificent tall girl who had danced all the afternoon. She was wearing a jasmine garland on her tight blue dress, wet with perspiration from the small of her back to her legs. She was laughing as she danced and throwing back her head. As she passed the tables, she left behind her a mingled scent of flowers and flesh. When evening came, I could no longer see her body pressed tight to her partner, but against the sky whirled alternating spots of white jasmine and black hair and when she would throw back her swelling breast, I would hear her laugh and see her partner's profile suddenly plunge forward. I owe to such evenings the idea I have of innocence. In any case I learn not to separate these creatures bursting with violent energy from the sky where their desires whirl.

In the neighbourhood movies in Algiers, peppermint lozenges are sometimes sold with, stamped in red, all that is necessary to the awakening of love: (1) questions: 'When will you marry me?' 'Do you love me?' and (2) replies: 'Madly', 'Next Spring'. After having prepared the way you pass them to your neighbour who answers likewise or else turns a deaf ear. At Belcourt marriages have been arranged this way and whole lives been pledged by the mere exchange of peppermint lozenges. And this really depicts the childlike people of this region.

The distinguishing mark of youth is perhaps a magnificent vocation for facile joys. But above all it is a haste to live that borders on waste. At Belcourt, as at Bab-el-Oued, people get married young. They go to work early and in ten years exhaust the experience of a lifetime. A thirty-year-old workman has already played all the cards in his hand. He awaits the end between his wife and his children. His joys have been sudden and merciless, as has been his life. One realizes that he is born of this country where everything is given to be taken away. In that plenty and profusion life follows the sweep of great passions, sudden, exacting, and generous. It is not to be built up but to be burned up. Stopping to think and becoming better are out of the question.

The notion of hell, for instance, is merely a funny joke here. Such imaginings are allowed only to the very virtuous. And I really think that virtue is a meaningless word in all Algeria. Not that these men lack principles. They have their code and a very special one. You are not disrespectful to your mother. You see that your wife is respected in the street. You show consideration for a pregnant woman. You don't double up on an adversary, because 'that looks bad'. Whoever does not observe these elementary commandments, 'is not a man', and the question is decided. This strikes me as fair and strong. There are still many of us who automatically observe this code of the street, the only disinterested one I know. But at the same time the shopkeeper's ethics are unknown. I have always seen faces around me filled with pity at the sight of a man between two policemen. And, before knowing whether the man had stolen, killed his father, or was merely a nonconformist, they would say: 'the poor fellow' or else, with a hint of admiration: 'he's a pirate, all right.'

There are races born for pride and life. They are the ones that nourish the strangest vocation for boredom. It is also among them that the attitude towards death is the most repulsive. Apart from sensual pleasure, the amusements of this race are among the silliest. A society of bowlers and association banquets, the three-franc movies and parish feasts have for years provided the recreation of those over thirty. Algiers Sundays are among the most sinister. How then could this race devoid of spirituality clothe in myths the profound horror of its life? Everything related to death is either ridiculous or hateful here. This populace without religion and without idols dies alone after having lived in a crowd. I know no more hideous spot than the cemetery on Boulevard Bru, opposite one of the most beautiful land-scapes in the world. An accumulation of bad taste among the black fencings allows a dreadful melancholy to rise from this spot where death shows her true likeness. 'Everything fades,' say the heart-shaped ex-votos, 'except memory.' And all insist on that paltry eternity provided us cheaply by the hearts of those who loved us. The same words fit all despairs. Addressed to the dead man, they speak to him in the second person (our memory will never forsake you); lugubrious pre-tence which attributes a body and desires to what is at best a black liquid. Elsewhere, amidst a deadly profusion of marble flowers and birds, this bold assertion: 'Never will your grave be without flowers.' But never fear: the inscription sur-rounds a gilded stucco bouquet, very time-saving for the living (like those *immortelles* which owe their pompous name to the gratitude of those who still jump on to moving buses). Inasmuch as it is essential to keep up with the times, the clas-sic warbler is sometimes replaced by an astounding pearl aeroplane piloted by a silly angel who, without regard for logic, is provided with an impressive pair of wings.

Yet how to bring out that these images of death are never separated from life? Here the values are closely linked. The favourite joke of Algerian undertakers, when driving an empty hearse, is to shout: 'Want a ride, sister?' to any pretty girls they meet on the way. There is no objection to seeing a symbol in this, even if somewhat untoward. It may seem blasphemous, likewise, to reply to the announcement of a death while winking one's left eye: 'Poor fellow, he'll never sing again,' or, like that woman of Oran who had never loved her husband: 'God gave him to me and God has taken him from me.' But, all in all, I see nothing sacred in death and am well aware, on the other hand, of the distance there is between fear and respect. Everything here suggests the horror of dying in a country that invites one to live. And yet it is under the very walls of this cemetery that the young of Belcourt have their assignations and that the girls offer themselves to kisses and caresses.

I am well aware that such a race cannot be accepted by all. Here intelligence has no place as in Italy. This race is indifferent to the mind. It has a cult for an admiration of the body. Whence its strength, its innocent cynicism, and puerile vanity which explains why it is so severely judged. It is commonly blamed for its 'mentality' – that is, a way of seeing and of living. And it is true that a certain intensity of life is inseparable from injustice. Yet here is a race without past, without tradition, and yet not without poetry – but a poetry whose quality I know well, harsh, carnal, far from tenderness, that of their very sky, the only one in truth to move me and bring me inner peace. The contrary of a civilized nation is a creative nation. I have the mad hope that, without knowing it perhaps, these barbarians lounging on beaches are actually modelling the image of a culture in which the greatness of man will at last find its true likeness. This race wholly cast into its present lives without myths, without solace. It has put all its possessions on this earth and therefore remains without defence against death. All the gifts of physical beauty have been lavished on it. And with them, the strange avidity that always accompanies that wealth without future. Everything that is done here shows a horror of stability and a disregard for the future. People are in haste to live and if an art were to be born here it would obey that hatred of permanence that made the Dorians fashion their first column in wood. And yet, yes, one can find measure as well as excess in the violent and keen face of this race, in this summer sky with nothing tender in it, before which all truths can be uttered and on which no deceptive divinity has traced the signs of hope or of redemption. Between this sky and these faces turned towards it, nothing on which to hang a mythology, a literature, an ethic or a religion, but stones, flesh, stars and those truths the hand can touch.

To feel one's attachment to a certain region, one's love for a certain group of men, to know that there is always a spot where one's heart will feel at peace – these are many certainties for a single human life. And yet this is not enough. But at certain moments everything yearns for that spiritual home. 'Yes, we must go back there – there, indeed.' Is there anything odd in finding on earth that union that Plotinus longed for? Unity is expressed here in terms of sun and sea. The heart is sensitive to it through a certain savour of flesh which constitutes its bitterness and its grandeur. I learn that there is no superhuman happiness, no eternity outside the sweep of days. These paltry and essential belongings, these relative truths are the only ones to stir me. As for the others, the 'ideal' truths, I have not enough soul to understand them. Not that one must be an animal, but I find no meaning in the happiness of angels. I know simply that this sky will last longer than I. And what shall I call eternity except what will continue after my death? I am not expressing here the creature's satisfaction with his condition. It is quite a different matter. It is not always easy to be a man, still less to be a pure man. But being pure is recovering that spiritual home where one can feel the world's relationship, where one's pulse-beats coincide with the violent throbbing of the two o'clock sun. It is well known that one's native land is always recognized at the moment of losing it. For those who are too uneasy about themselves, their native land is the one that negates them. I should not like to be brutal or seem extravagant. But after all, what negates me in this life is first what kills me. Everything that exalts life at the same time increases its absurdity. In the Algerian summer I learn that one thing only is more tragic than suffering and that is the life of a happy man. But it may be also the way to a greater life because it leads to not cheating.

Many, in fact, feign love of life to evade love itself. They try their skill at enjoyment and at 'indulging in experiences'. But this is illusory. It requires a rare vocation to be a sensualist. The life of a man is fulfilled without the aid of his mind, with its backward and forward movements, at one and the same time its solitude and its presences. To see these men of Belcourt working, protecting their wives and children, and often without a reproach, I think one can feel a secret shame. To be sure, I have no illusions about it. There is not much love in the lives I am speaking of. I ought to say that not much remains. But at least they have evaded nothing. There are words I have never really understood, such as 'sin'. Yet I believe these men have never sinned against life. For if there is a sin against life, it consists perhaps not so much in despairing of life as in hoping for another life and in eluding the implacable grandeur of this life. These men have not cheated. Gods of summer they were at twenty by their enthusiasm for life and they still are, deprived of all hope. I have seen two of them die. They were full of horror, but silent. It is better thus. From Pandora's box, where all the ills of humanity swarmed, the Greeks drew out hope after all the others, as the most dreadful of all. I know no more stirring symbol; for, contrary to the general belief, hope equals resignation. And to live is not to resign oneself.

This at least is the bitter lesson of Algerian summers. But already the season is wavering and summer totters. The first September rains, after such violence and hardening, are like the liberated earth's first tears, as if for a few days this country tried its hand at tenderness. Yet at the same period the carob-trees cover all of Algeria with a scent of love. In the evening or after the rain, the whole earth, its womb moist with a seed redolent of bitter almond, rests after having given herself to the sun all summer long. And again that scent hallows the union of man and earth and awakens in us the only really virile love in this world: ephemeral and noble.

Albert Camus
100 years

'Man cannot do without beauty'
Albert Camus

Discover Albert Camus in his centenary year

The Adulterous Woman
Caligula and Other Plays
Exile and the Kingdom
The Fall
The First Man
A Happy Death
The Myth of Sisyphus
The Outsider
The Plague
The Rebel
Selected Essays and Notebooks

www.penguinclassics.com